COOKING
with CHOCOLATE

MORE THAN 70 ENTRÉES, DRINKS, AND DECADENT DESSERTS

This 2007 edition is published by Gramercy Books, an imprint of
Random House Value Publishing, a division of Random House, Inc.,
New York, by arrangement with Penn Publishing Ltd..

Gramercy is a registered trademark and the colophon is a trademark
of Random House, Inc.

Random House
New York • Toronto • London • Sydney • Auckland
www.randomhouse.com

Printed and bound in China.

Edited by Sorelle Weinstein
Interior design by Eddie Goldfine
Layout by Ariane Rybski

A catalog record for this title is available from the Library of Congress.

ISBN: 978-0-517-22941-5

10 9 8 7 6 5 4 3 2 1

COOKING
with CHOCOLATE

MORE THAN 70 ENTRÉES, DRINKS, AND DECADENT DESSERTS

AVNER LASKIN

Photography by
DANYA WEINER

GRAMERCY BOOKS
NEW YORK

TABLE OF
CONTENTS

INTRODUCTION

I admit it—I am addicted to chocolate. Chocolate does not just stimulate the taste buds, but all our senses. Chocolate evokes passion and desire and symbolizes the potency of love. Chocolate conveys a message of celebration, love, friendship, and even forgiveness.

Over the years, I have worked in numerous kitchens and have experimented with many bold and innovative techniques in cooking, but the truth is that I have always been intimidated by the thought of working with, and writing about, chocolate. I have written several different cookbooks and did not flinch at the prospect of writing about bread, pastries, and ice cream. But chocolate has always been placed on a pedestal, enticing but out of my reach. Finally, my love of chocolate and my curiosity overcame my reluctance, and in writing this cookbook, I embarked upon a sensual and deeply satisfying journey, which I hope you too will enjoy.

The possibilities of chocolate are endless. Chocolate can be a hot drink on a cold day, a cold drink on a hot day, a thick cake, a creamy ice cream, or a decadent confectionary. It can be cooked, baked, whipped, and frothed. It can be used in frying, coating, steaming, and melting. It can be served soft, hard, hot, or cold. It is deliciously sweet as milk chocolate and impressively sophisticated as bittersweet chocolate. Chocolate is marvelous in all forms and on any occasion.

It is hard to believe that until the 16th century, the cocoa tree and its miraculous beans were a secret known only to the Mayans and Aztecs. When the marvelous product finally reached Europe in the mid-1500s, it was prohibitively expensive and difficult to obtain. Only the wealthy could afford the indulgence. Not only that, but chocolate was only available in the form of a bitter beverage. The potential for sauces, cakes, soufflés, trifles, pralines, cookies, and ice cream went unrealized for years!

Thankfully, chocolate is no longer just a dessert. In its raw, unsweetened form, chocolate can be used to season meat, poultry, and fish. Chocolate is now an aperitif, an appetizer, a first course and an entrée. Chocolate is being combined with such ingredients as pork, chicken, goose, and pasta to create culinary masterpieces.

Cooking with Chocolate includes more than 70 recipes, all of which contain chocolate as a main ingredient. Before trying out a recipe, make sure to read the chapter on Essentials; the guidelines and instructions contained in these pages are vital in order to successfully implement the recipes.

Whether you are searching for a quick and easy dessert, wish to experiment with a daring entrée, or simply want to cuddle up on a cold winter's night with a mug of soothing hot chocolate, you will be sure to find a perfect recipe in the following seven sections within this book.

In **Entreés**, you'll learn how to create adventurous and sumptuous main courses with exciting chocolate sauces and marinades. **Cakes** will teach you how to recreate the wonderfully rich and creamy chocolate cakes that are normally found only on the dessert cart in a five-star restaurant. The chapter on **Baked Treats** presents my favorite recipes for preparing fine chocolate patisserie. In **Desserts**, you will find divine recipes for chocolate creations that will satisfy any sweet tooth. One of my favorite chapters is **Pralines and Truffles.** In it, you will learn how to prepare gorgeous chocolate confections that are perfect to give as gifts or simply to treat yourself. Finally, the chapter **Cold and Hot Drinks** will bring you instant relief and pleasure when it is freezing outside and you yearn for something hot, or when it is a scorching hot summer's day and you need a cool refresher.

This book comes with a warning: if you aren't already addicted to chocolate, you will be after flipping through pages and pages of mouthwatering and alluring pictures. **Cooking with Chocolate** is more than just a cookbook; it is a feast for the imagination and the soul.

Avner Laskin

ESSENTIALS

Chocolate is made from cocoa beans, which are harvested, dried, wrapped in banana leaves to ferment, and then shipped to manufacturers all over the world. To make chocolate, the fermented beans are roasted and ground to produce chocolate "liquor." The liquor is made up of 50 percent cocoa solids and 50 percent cocoa butter. Finished chocolate is either made into bars by adding various ingredients like sugar, milk, and palm oil, or cocoa powder, which requires the removal of the cocoa butter from the liquor. The quality of the chocolate that is produced is determined by the concentration of cocoa solids in the finished product.

When you follow the recipes described in the chapters that follow, it is important to make use of the best chocolate you can find. For best results, melt chocolate in a double boiler. Keep the water in the bottom pot at a steady simmer, and do not allow it to touch the underside of the top pot. Stir only at the end. If you don't have a double boiler, you can achieve the same results by placing the chocolate pieces in a bowl over a pan of simmering water.

Below, I will tell you which chocolate is best suited for use in each chapter.

ENTREÉS
For entrées, I recommend that you use chocolate that contains at least 70 percent cocoa solids. With such a high concentration of cocoa solids, the bitterness of the chocolate enhances the flavor of these entrées. Similarly, using chocolate that is high in cocoa butter is also recommended as it will thicken our sauces and give them a regal glossiness suitable for the majesty of our chocolate creations. You may also use milk chocolate or white chocolate in these recipes.

CAKES
Chocolate that contains 60 percent cocoa solids is best for baking these delicious cakes. You may use chocolate that is up to 80 percent cocoa solids; however, if you choose to use chocolate with a higher concentration, it is best to increase the amount of sugar by one third in order to counteract the bitterness of the cocoa. You may also use milk chocolate or white chocolate in these recipes.

BAKED TREATS
For these tasty treats it is best to use chocolate with 60 percent cocoa solids. As with cakes, you may use chocolate that is up to 80 percent cocoa solids, but if you do, remember to increase the amount of sugar in the recipe by one third in order to counteract the bitterness of the cocoa.

DESSERTS
Because of the nature of these desserts, any quality chocolate will suffice. You may use higher than 60 percent cocoa solids, but remember to increase the amount of sugar in the recipe by one third or these desserts will be too bitter.

PRALINES AND TRUFFLES
For these confections, you may use chocolate that is up to 80 percent cocoa solids for the coating and chocolate that is up 60 percent cocoa solids

for use in the filling. You may also use milk chocolate or white chocolate for creating these candy delights.

CHOCOLATE DRINKS

For hot chocolate drinks, you should either use chocolate that has no more than 60 percent cocoa solids or milk chocolate. For cold drinks as well, it is best not to use chocolate that contains higher than 60 percent concentration of cocoa solids. For these recipes, however, you can use any type of chocolate that appeals to you.

Before you begin cooking, it is very important that you read through a recipe from beginning to end. Familiarize yourself with the ingredients and make sure that you have the proper amounts for the recipe. You should also be sure that you have the proper tools to create your culinary masterpiece. Quality cooking and baking supplies are available on the Internet and at chef supply stores at reasonable prices. Any investment you make in high quality tools for your recipes will pay off in the high quality of your cooking.

BAKING PANS AND TOOLS

I always recommend using nonstick or silicone baking pans because they are the easiest to clean and require less greasing. The pans we'll be using are:

Madeleine pan for making scallop-shaped mini-cakes. These specialty baking moulds are used for traditional Madeleines or any batter cake recipe.

Cake collars to line the inside of baking rings. These 2 x 28.5 inch transparent cellophane collars are used to protect the edges of mousse and cream cakes. They allow for easier removal of the cake from the baking ring. Remember to remove the collar before defrosting the cakes.

Individual tube pans for making individual desserts. These should be Teflon-coated or made from silicone.

Praline moulds to create pralines. Plastic praline moulds come in a wide variety of shapes and sizes and are available on the Internet and at chef supply stores. It is important to choose shapes that complement the finished pralines. For example, chocolate-covered cherries should be made in moulds that are deep enough to hold a whole cherry.

Parchment paper for lining pans and baking sheets. The parchment also can be used to protect cakes that contain layers of mousse or cream. Parchment paper is available in both sheets and rolls. I recommend using sheets, since they are larger and do not curl.

Pastry brush to brush gloss on baked goods. These brushes should ideally be long bristled because a longer bristle is softer and will not damage the pastry.

Good quality whisk for beating and emulsifying ingredients. A strong whisk is perfect for mixing ingredients when using an electric mixer would cause unnecessary agitation of the mixture.

Wide rubber or silicone spatula for mixing and folding. Wider spatulas are ideal for getting to the bottom of a mixing bowl and will help you mix your ingredients more thoroughly. Also, when folding ingredients into a recipe it is essential to use a good spatula.

Candy thermometer for measuring the temperature of food. A thermometer that measures above 400°F will keep your caramel from burning and also allows you to monitor delicate praline and truffle recipes that require a precise temperature for best results.

Measuring cups and spoons for accurate measurements.

Long handled wooden spoon for mixing. You can use the handle of a wooden spoon to form the Chocolate Tuile Cookies (page 66).

Ceramic pie weights to weigh down flaky crusts. When baking pies or quiche shells, it is important to prevent the crusts from bubbling up when pre-baking before filling. Ceramic weights are more hygienic than metal weights. You may also use dried beans or rice on top of a piece of parchment paper instead of pie weights. Be sure to discard them after use.

4-inch stainless steel spatula for general use. A metal spatula can be used to make chocolate curls, to scrape dough from a kneading board, or to pick up ingredients from a flat work surface.

12-inch palette knife with a rounded top to spread creamy ingredients and frosting. A good palette knife is especially useful for working with pastry batter and mousse.

20-inch pastry bag for piping dough or frosting.

I prefer this length of pastry bag because it is large enough to hold a generous amount of material and strong enough that it never leaks. Use a silicone pastry bag, if possible, since they are easier to clean, do not stain, and do not absorb odors or flavor like cloth pastry bags.

Stainless steel pastry tip set for use with the pastry bag. A good set of pastry tips will provide you with all the sizes and shapes that you will need for the recipes in this book. Pastry tips are available on the Internet and in chef supply stores. Stainless steel is easy to clean and will not stain.

Cooling rack for cooling hot bakery. A metal cooling rack is absolutely essential for moving, storing, and cooling pastries and other baked goods.

Fondue forks for dipping fruit, candy, or cookies in chocolate fondue.

ELECTRICAL EQUIPMENT

Standing electric mixer with attachments for mixing cake batter, beating eggs, and thoroughly blending ingredients.

Food processor with steel blade to chop, grate, and crush ingredients. A good food processor with a baking hook can also be used to knead dough for certain recipes.

Ice cream machine for making homemade ice cream.

BASIC RECIPES

TORTE PASTRY

MAKES ENOUGH FOR TWO 10-INCH CAKES

4 eggs, separated

2/3 cup sugar

1/2 cup flour

1. In an electric mixer, beat the egg whites until they turn into a creamy foam.

2. Gradually add half the sugar and continue beating until it forms stiff peaks.

3. In a separate bowl, beat the yolks with remaining sugar until foamy and soft. Fold the flour into the beaten egg yolks using a rubber spatula. Mix gently until smooth.

4. Fold the egg whites into the egg yolk mixture using a rubber spatula and mix gently until smooth and uniform. Use immediately.

For pistachio torte pastry, add 1/2 cup of coarsely crushed pistachios when you fold in the flour.

COCOA TORTE PASTRY

MAKES ENOUGH FOR TWO 10-INCH CAKES

4 eggs, separated

1/2 cup sugar

1/2 cup flour

2 tablespoons premium cocoa

1. In an electric mixer, beat the egg whites until they turn into a creamy foam.

2. Gradually add 1/4 cup sugar and continue beating until it forms stiff peaks.

3. In a separate bowl, beat the yolks and the remaining 1/4 cup of sugar until foamy and soft. Fold the flour and the cocoa into the beaten egg yolks using a rubber spatula. Mix gently until smooth.

4. Fold the egg whites into the egg yolk mixture using a rubber spatula and mix gently until smooth and uniform. Use immediately.

CHOCOLATE ALMOND CRISP PASTRY

MAKES ENOUGH FOR TWO 10-INCH CAKES

1/2 cup chilled butter

1/4 cup powdered sugar

1/4 cup bleached almonds, crushed

1 egg

1/2 cup water

1/2 teaspoon salt

1 cup flour

2 tablespoons premium cocoa

1. Place the butter and half the powdered sugar in a food processor and process for 2 minutes until you get a smooth dough.

2. Turn off the food processor and add the almonds and the remaining powdered sugar. Process for 2 minutes until the dough is smooth.

3. Turn off the processor and add the egg, water, salt, half the flour, and the cocoa. Process for 2 more minutes until the dough is smooth and uniform. Add the remaining flour and continue to process until the dough forms a ball.

4. Remove the ball of dough from the food processor and wrap it in plastic wrap. Refrigerate for at least 1 hour before using.

Note: You can freeze this dough for up to 2 months. To defrost, remove from the freezer and let stand at room temperature.

ROYAL CHOCOLATE FROSTING

PREPARES AROUND 4 CUPS, ENOUGH FROSTING FOR TWO 10-INCH ROUND CAKES

1/2 cup water

1/2 cup sugar

10 ounces bittersweet chocolate, finely chopped

2 tablespoons vegetable oil

1/4 cup glucose

1 cup heavy cream

1. In a small saucepan, combine the water and the sugar and bring to a boil. Do not stir while the syrup is boiling. Once the syrup has boiled, remove from the flame and set aside.

2. Melt the chocolate in the top of a double boiler. Be careful not to allow the chocolate to come into contact with the boiling syrup.

3. When the chocolate has melted, add the oil and glucose and mix well.

4. Add the cream and mix well.

5. Pour the syrup into the melted chocolate mixture and remove from the heat. Mix well. You may use it immediately or let it cool and store it covered in the refrigerator for up to 2 weeks. In order to use the frosting after it has been refrigerated, you may warm the frosting in a double boiler before using.

NOUGATINE

1. Preheat oven to 400°F.

2. Place the hazelnuts in a pan and bake for 12 minutes or until the shells are browned.

3. Remove from the oven and pour the nuts onto a kitchen towel. Wrap the towel around the nuts and rub them together until the shells fall off.

4. Transfer the shelled hazelnuts to a food processor and grind them with a round metal blade until they form a smooth mixture.

5. Add the powdered sugar and the butter and process until they form a golden brown paste.

6. Remove from the food processor and transfer the paste to a sealed container. You may store the nougatine for up to 1 month in the refrigerator.

MUSCADINE

1. Combine all the ingredients in a medium saucepan and heat over a medium flame until they form a golden brown caramel.

2. Grease a baking sheet with cooking oil and pour the almond caramel onto the tray. Spread the mixture evenly with a wooden spoon and let it cool at room temperature for 1 hour.

3. After the almonds have cooled, transfer to a food processor and process with a round metal blade until the mixture is the texture of breadcrumbs.

4. Transfer to a sealed container and store in a cool dark place. You can store the muscadine for up to 1 week.

1
ENTRÉES

UOVA AL MAIS E CIOCCOLATO AMARO

SERVES 4

1/4 cup butter

1/2 pound canned corn, drained of liquid

1/2 teaspoon salt

16 strips smoked bacon

8 eggs

1/4 cup bittersweet chocolate, grated

TOOLS
Heavy cast iron skillet or griddle

Bacon and eggs made even better with bittersweet chocolate and sweet corn.

1. Melt the butter in a large non-stick skillet over a medium flame.
2. Add the corn and sauté until lightly browned.
3. Add the salt and mix well. Transfer to a clean bowl and set aside.
4. Using the same skillet, sauté the bacon until it is golden brown.
5. Pour the eggs on the bacon in the skillet and cook until the yolks solidify.
6. Place the corn on a large serving plate.
7. Set the eggs and bacon on top of the corn and sprinkle the grated chocolate on top.
8. Serve hot.

CHOCOLATE CHILI SPARE RIBS

SERVES 6

3 ounces bittersweet chocolate, grated

2 tablespoons mole poblano sauce (Mexican chili sauce)

1 clove garlic, chopped

Zest of 1 orange

1/2 cup orange juice

1 tablespoon citrus liqueur

3 tablespoons melted butter

1/2 teaspoon salt

2 pounds fresh pork spare ribs

Mole poblano derives from the Puebla region in Mexico. It is a famous chili sauce, combining chiles, nuts, and chocolate.

1. Preheat the oven to 400°F.
2. Melt the chocolate in the top of a double boiler.
3. Remove from the heat. Add the mole poblano sauce, garlic, orange zest, orange juice, citrus liqueur, melted butter, and salt. Mix well.
4. Place the spare ribs in the chocolate mixture and coat well. Refrigerate for 30 minutes. At this stage, you can store the ribs for up to 24 hours in the refrigerator.
5. Arrange the spare ribs on a baking sheet and cover with aluminum foil. Bake for 40 minutes at 400°F.
6. Remove the ribs from the oven and remove the foil. Bake for 15 minutes uncovered.
7. Remove from the oven and serve immediately with the pan juices. Alternatively, this dish can be stored in the refrigerator overnight before serving the next day.

MEXICAN ROAST CHICKEN IN CHOCOLATE MARINADE

The word "mole" comes from the Nahuatl word mulli, which means "sauce" or "mixture".

1. Preheat the oven to 400°F.

2. In a large bowl, combine the mole poblano sauce, chocolate, garlic, oil, salt, and chili and mix well.

3. Rub the chocolate and spice mixture all over the chicken.

4. Place the chicken breast side down in a deep roasting pan. Cook in the oven for 30 minutes.

5. Turn the chicken on its side and cook for 15 minutes.

6. Turn the chicken on the other side and cook for 15 minutes.

7. Turn the chicken so it is breast up in the pan and cook for 15 minutes.

8. Remove the chicken from the oven and transfer to a serving tray.

GOOSE LIVER WITH CHOCOLATE BRANDY SAUCE

This dish is excellent served as a first course for any gourmet meal.

1. In a small saucepan, bring the wine to a boil. Add the cream and cook for 10 minutes over a low flame.

2. Add the chocolate, brandy, and salt, and cook until thick and smooth.

3. Remove from the heat. Add the butter and mix well. Set aside.

4. Heat the skillet on a low flame.

5. While the skillet is heating, slice the liver into 1/2-inch slices. Sprinkle both sides of the slices of liver with the pepper and coarse salt.

6. Place the liver on the griddle without oil and grill for no longer than 2 minutes on each side.

7. Transfer the liver to a serving plate and pour the sauce over it. Serve immediately.

CHICKEN TERRINE WITH COLD CHOCOLATE SAUCE

Prepare a day in advance and the flavors will be superb.

SERVES 6

1 pound fresh chicken liver

1 tablespoon brandy

1/2 teaspoon salt

1/2 teaspoon ground white pepper

1/4 cup butter

FOR THE SAUCE

5 ounces bittersweet chocolate

1 tablespoon Mole Paste (Mexican spice mixture paste)

1/2 teaspoon salt

1 cup white dessert wine

TOOLS

10-inch terrine pan

Plastic wrap

Heavy cast iron skillet

Aluminum foil

1. Preheat the oven to 325°F.

2. Prepare the terrine pan by lining the pan with plastic wrap. Use enough wrap so that there is extra on each side which can be wrapped over the top to cover the terrine when it is prepared.

3. Place the liver, brandy, salt, and pepper in a large bowl. Mix well and refrigerate for 30 minutes.

4. Heat the skillet on a medium flame. Melt the butter in the skillet. Place the livers in the skillet and lightly fry until the liver turns light grey. Remove from heat.

5. Place the livers in the terrine pan and press them into the bottom of the pan with the back of a spoon.

6. Cover the pan with the plastic wrap.

7. Cover the pan with aluminum foil and cook in the oven for 45 minutes at 325°F.

8. Remove the terrine and let cool on a metal cooling rack. Refrigerate overnight.

9. The next day, melt the chocolate in the top of a double boiler. When the chocolate is melted, remove from the heat and add the mole paste, salt, and wine and mix well.

10. Remove the terrine from the refrigerator and remove the plastic wrap. Slice the liver into 1/2-inch thick slices.

11. To serve, place two slices of terrine on a bed of green lettuce and pour a tablespoon of sauce on top. Serve immediately.

PORK FILLET IN CHOCOLATE AND SPICES

SERVES 4

1/2 cup beef stock or 1 tablespoon beef stock powder mixed with 1/2 cup water

4 ounces bittersweet chocolate

2 tablespoons butter

1/2 cup fresh mushrooms, sliced thinly

2 tablespoons olive oil

Pinch of salt

2 cloves garlic, chopped

1 tablespoon thyme

1 cup steamed white rice

1 whole pork fillet (around 3/4 pound)

1 teaspoon ground black pepper

1/2 teaspoon salt

TOOLS
Large skillet

Baking sheet

A unique take on a traditional Sunday dinner.

1. Preheat the oven to 450°F.

2. In a small saucepan bring the beef stock to a boil. When the stock has boiled, add the chocolate and cook until the sauce is thick.

3. Remove from the heat. Add the butter and mix well. Set aside.

4. In a large skillet on a high flame, sauté the mushrooms, olive oil, salt, garlic, and half the thyme. Stir well while sautéing.

5. When the mushrooms are soft, add the rice to the skillet. Mix well and cook for 3 minutes while stirring.

6. Place the pork fillet on a baking sheet. Sprinkle the rest of the thyme, ground pepper, and salt. Press the spices into the fillet so they stick well.

7. Bake for 10 minutes.

8. Remove the fillet from the oven and transfer to a cutting board. Wait 2 minutes and slice the fillet into 1/4-inch thick slices using a sharp chef's knife.

9. Place two or three spoons of rice in the center of a serving tray and arrange the pork fillet on top. Pour the sauce on the side and serve immediately.

ROAST GOOSE WITH CHOCOLATE SAUCE

SERVES 4

1/2 cup chicken stock or 1 tablespoon chicken soup powder mixed with 1 cup water

3 ounces bittersweet chocolate

2 tablespoons butter

1/2 teaspoon salt

1/2 teaspoon cumin seeds

1/2 teaspoon coriander seeds

1/2 teaspoon ground black pepper

1/2 teaspoon coarse salt

2 slices of moulard breast or goose breast

TOOLS
Heavy cast iron skillet or griddle

Spice mill, mortar and pestle, or food processor to grind spices

Goose breast typically has a thick layer of fat. Cooked properly, the breast will be moist and the fatty layer crispy but not greasy.

1. Preheat the oven to 400°F.

2. In a small saucepan, bring the chicken stock to a boil. Add the chocolate and cook until the chocolate is melted.

3. Remove from the heat. Add the butter and salt. Mix well and set aside.

4. Heat the skillet on a high flame.

5. While the skillet is heating, place the cumin, coriander, black pepper, and coarse salt in the spice mill or food processor. Grind the spices until they form a uniform mixture.

6. With a sharp knife, make a slit in the fatty part of the breast. Rub the spice mixture over the whole poultry breast.

7. Place the breasts on the skillet without oil and grill each breast for no longer than 3 minutes on each side.

8. Transfer the breasts to a baking pan and bake in the oven for 5 minutes at 400 °F.

9. Remove from the oven and transfer to a cutting board. With a sharp knife, slice 1/4-inch thick slices from each breast and arrange on a serving plate. Drizzle the sauce over the strips of breast and serve.

10. Serve with fried Asian noodles.

CHOCOLATE TERIYAKI CHICKEN WINGS

Mole paste can be bought ready-made from local Mexican markets or supermarkets. It is a traditional Mexican spice mixture that is used in a variety of dishes.

SERVES 5

3 ounces bittersweet chocolate, grated

2 tablespoons sweet chili sauce

1 tablespoon mole paste (Mexican spice mixture paste)

1 clove garlic, chopped

2 tablespoons teriyaki sauce

3 tablespoons melted butter

30 chicken wings, cleaned

1. Preheat the oven to 425°F.

2. Melt the chocolate in the top of a double boiler.

3. Remove from the heat and add the sweet chili sauce, mole paste, garlic, teriyaki sauce, and the melted butter. Mix well.

4. Place the chicken wings in the bowl with the chocolate mixture, mix well and refrigerate for 30 minutes. At this stage, you can store the wings in the refrigerator for up to 24 hours.

5. After the chicken has marinated for at least 30 minutes, arrange the wings in a baking pan and cook for 10 minutes at 425°F.

6. After 10 minutes, turn the wings so that the uncooked side faces up. Cook for another 12 minutes.

7. Remove the wings from the oven, arrange them on a serving plate, and serve immediately as an appetizer or as a first course.

LAMB CASSEROLE WITH RED WINE AND CHOCOLATE

Prepare this casserole one day before serving and give the flavors a chance to blend together and become rich and tasty.

SERVES 6

3 tablespoons extra virgin olive oil

2 pounds boneless leg of lamb, cut into 1-inch pieces

1 teaspoon coarse salt

1 teaspoon ground black pepper

1 medium-sized red onion, finely chopped

6 cloves garlic, chopped

3 medium carrots, peeled and chopped into 1/2 -inch pieces

1 bottle dry red wine

1 tablespoon thyme

5 ounces bittersweet chocolate

1 sprig rosemary

TOOLS
Large cast iron casserole pot with lid

1. Preheat the oven to 400°F.

2. Heat the casserole dish on a medium flame and add the olive oil.

3. Rub the meat with 1/2 teaspoon salt and the black pepper. Place the meat in the casserole pot and brown 2 minutes on each side. Remove the meat and set aside.

4. Add the onion, garlic, carrots, and 1/2 teaspoon salt to the pot and sauté for 5 minutes while stirring.

5. Add the wine and the thyme and bring to a boil. When the liquid is boiling, add the chocolate and mix well until it is completely melted.

6. Add the browned meat and the rosemary. Cover the pot and cook at 400°F for 1 1/2 hours.

7. After 1 1/2 hours, uncover the casserole and cook for another 30 minutes.

8. Serve immediately or you may store in the refrigerator until the next day. Serve with steamed rice or mashed potatoes.

STEAK WITH CHOCOLATE AND CHILI SAUCE

Use a good cut of beef for a steak that is tender and juicy and one that will be worthy of the spicy chocolate sauce.

1. In a small saucepan, bring the beef stock to a boil. When the stock is boiling, add the chocolate and cook together until the chocolate is melted. Add the cream and continue to cook for 3 minutes.

2. Remove the sauce from the heat. Add the butter, brandy, salt, and the chili. Mix well and set aside.

3. Heat the skillet on a high flame.

4. While the skillet is heating, sprinkle the black pepper and the coarse salt on both sides of the steaks.

5. Place the steaks on the hot skillet without any oil. Grill the steaks for 3-5 minutes on each side or until done as desired.

6. Transfer the steaks to a serving plate and pour the sauce over them.

7. Serve immediately with roasted red potatoes, steamed asparagus, or any attractive side dish.

SERVES 4

1/2 cup beef stock or
1 tablespoon powdered
beef stock mixed with
1/2 cup water

4 ounces bittersweet
chocolate

1/4 cup heavy cream

2 tablespoons butter

1 tablespoon brandy

1/2 teaspoon salt

1/2 teaspoon fresh red
chili, finely chopped

4 beef steaks, entrecote
or porterhouse

1 teaspoon ground
black pepper

1/2 teaspoon coarse salt

TOOLS
Heavy cast iron skillet
or griddle

CHICKEN SATAY

SERVES 4

3 ounces grated bittersweet chocolate

2 tablespoons sweet chili sauce

1 clove garlic, chopped

3 tablespoons peanut butter

2 tablespoons melted butter

1 tablespoon soy sauce

4 tablespoons peanuts, crushed

3/4 pound boneless chicken thighs

TOOLS
12 short bamboo skewers

An Asian delight with a chocolate twist.

1. Preheat the oven to 425°F.

2. Melt the chocolate in the top of a double boiler.

3. Remove the melted chocolate from the heat and add the sweet chili sauce, garlic, peanut butter, melted butter, soy sauce, and 2 tablespoons of the crushed peanuts. Mix well.

4. Cut the chicken into 1/2-inch strips with a sharp knife. Add the chicken strips to the chocolate mixture and let them marinate for 30 minutes.

5. After the chicken has marinated, place the chicken strips on the skewers and arrange in a baking pan. At this stage, you can store the kabobs in the refrigerator for up to 24 hours.

6. Roast the chicken kabobs in the oven at 425°F for 6 minutes.

7. Turn the skewers so the uncooked side is face up and cook for another 5 minutes.

8. Remove from the oven and arrange on a serving plate. Sprinkle the remaining crushed peanuts on the kabobs to garnish. Serve immediately as an appetizer or as a first course.

TEMPURA SHRIMP WITH SPICY CHOCOLATE SAUCE

This dish is suitable for a first course, party, or cocktail hour.

SERVES 4

1/4 cup tempura mix

2/3 cup cold water

2 tablespoons sweet chili sauce

3 ounces bittersweet chocolate, grated

2 tablespoons fresh lemon juice

2 tablespoons Thai fish sauce

1 tablespoon melted butter

1 clove garlic, chopped

1 tablespoon fresh ginger, grated

3 cups of cooking oil

30 pieces jumbo shrimp, peeled and cleaned

TOOLS
Individual dishes for serving sauce, one for each diner

1. Place the tempura mix in a large bowl and gradually add the water. Whisk well until the mixture is smooth and of the same consistency as pancake batter. If the mixture is too thick, add more water, and if the mixture is too thin, add more tempura mix.

2. Place the chili sauce, chocolate, lemon juice, fish sauce, melted butter, garlic, and ginger in a large bowl. Mix well.

3. Pour cooking oil into a deep frying pan. Heat the oil. Hold the shrimp by the tail, dip them into the tempura mix, and coat well. Gently shake off the excess batter and fry the shrimp in the oil until they are golden brown.

4. Transfer the shrimp to a plate lined with paper towels. Use the towels to soak up the excess oil from frying. Transfer to a serving plate and place a dish of sauce in front of each diner.

2
CAKES

BLACK FOREST CAKE

SERVES 10

1/2 cocoa torte pastry (see Basic Recipes on page 11)

2 cups heavy cream

1 cup bittersweet chocolate, chopped into small pieces

2 cups fresh pitted cherries

2 tablespoons kirsch or other fruit liqueur

1/2 cup of sugar

TOOLS

2 baking sheets

Parchment paper

Pastry bag with 1/4-inch round tip

10-inch baking ring

Cellophane collar

This rich chocolate cake is enhanced by a hint of cherry liqueur, and the addition of fresh cherries gives an exhilarating burst of flavor.

1. Preheat the oven to 350°F. Line the baking sheets with parchment paper.

2. Fill the pastry bag with the cocoa torte pastry.

3. Pipe two rounds of the unbaked pastry, 10 inches in diameter each, on the baking sheets, starting from the outside working inwards. Bake for 20 minutes. Remove the baked pastry rounds along with the parchment and place them on a wire rack to cool for at least 30 minutes.

4. While the pastry is cooling, prepare the ganache in a small saucepan. Bring 1 cup of the cream to a boil. While the cream is boiling, place the chopped chocolate in a large mixing bowl. Remove the cream from the heat and pour it over the chocolate. Whisk together the cream and the melted chocolate until the mixture is smooth. Set aside.

5. Place the cherries in a bowl and pour the kirsch over them. Set aside for half an hour.

6. Turn the baked pastry over so that the parchment is facing upwards. Remove the parchment slowly and carefully so as not to break the pastry. (If the pastry breaks you can repair it later.)

7. Set the baking ring onto the baking sheet which will go into the freezer and line it with the cellophane collar. Carefully set one of the pastry rounds in the bottom of the ring with the side of the round that was covered by parchment facing up. Put the sheet in the freezer.

8. Prepare the mousse. Whip the remaining cream and sugar with an electric mixer until it forms soft peaks. Pour the cool ganache into the whipped cream and, using a rubber spatula, mix well until smooth.

9. Take the pastry out of the freezer and pour half the cherries into the ring. Layer half of the mousse on top of the cherries. Place the second pastry round on top of the mousse. Return to the freezer for 20 minutes.

10. Remove the cake from the freezer and pour the remaining cherries on top. With a frosting spatula or large flat knife, spread more mousse on top of the cherries. Transfer the remaining mousse to a pastry bag and dot the top of the cake with drops of mousse. Return to the freezer for 2 hours.

11. Before serving, remove the baking ring and let the cake sit at room temperature for 30 minutes. This cake can be stored in the refrigerator for up to 2 days.

CHOCOLATE TORTE

The center of this beautiful torte is decorated with chocolate curls and contrasts deliciously with the crunchy almond pastry base.

1. Roll out the pastry on a floured work surface until it is 1/8-inch thick.

2. Place the pastry carefully in the tart pan and press down with your fingers until the pastry is sitting firmly in the pan. Trim the excess pastry from the edges of the pan. You may gather the excess dough, roll it into a ball, wrap it well with plastic wrap, and store it in the freezer for up to 1 month.

3. Put the pastry into the freezer for 15 minutes and heat the oven to 375°F.

4. Cut a section of the parchment the same size as the bottom of the tart pan. Place the parchment in the pan on top of the pastry. Set the baking weights on top of the parchment and bake the pastry for 20 minutes.

5. Remove the baking weights and the parchment. Brush the pastry and the edges with the beaten egg and bake for 3 more minutes. Remove the baked pastry from the oven and let it cool to room temperature on a metal cooling rack.

6. In a small saucepan, bring the cream to a boil over a medium flame.

7. Remove the cream from the heat and add 9 ounces of the chopped chocolate. Mix well with a wooden spoon or a small whisk until the mixture is smooth. While you are stirring, add the brandy.

8. Pour the mixture into the pastry shell and put it in the refrigerator uncovered for 1 hour.

9. Melt the remaining 4 ounces of chocolate in the top of a double boiler.

10. With a plastic spatula, thinly spread the melted chocolate on the back of a backing sheet and put it in the refrigerator for 10 minutes or until the chocolate hardens but is not brittle.

11. Insert a spatula at a 45° angle into the chocolate and push forward to form chocolate curls. Repeat until there are enough curls to cover the top of the cake.

12. Carefully remove the tart from the refrigerator. Using a toothpick or small skewer, decorate the tart with the chocolate curls. This cake can be stored in the refrigerator for up to 2 days.

CHOCOLATE HAZELNUT CHEESECAKE

The combination of chocolate and hazelnuts creates a delicious accent for the velvety texture of this superb cheesecake.

1. Preheat the oven to 325°F.

2. Melt the chocolate and butter in the top of a double boiler.

3. Beat the egg whites and half the sugar (3/4 cup) with an electric mixer until they form stiff peaks. Set aside.

4. In a bowl, mix together the cheese, orange juice, and orange zest until the mixture is smooth and combined. Set aside.

5. When the chocolate is melted, remove the bowl from the boiling water. Mix in the hazelnuts. It is important to mix in the nuts well in order to cool the chocolate slightly.

6. After the chocolate-nut mixture is slightly cooled, add the egg yolks and mix well.

7. Pour the chocolate-nut mixture into the bowl with the cheese. Add the corn starch and mix well until the mixture is combined.

8. Fold in the beaten egg whites until the mixture is combined.

9. Pour the mixture into the baking pan and bake for 40 minutes.

10. After baking, let the cake cool for 1 hour and then refrigerate for 2 hours. The cake will break apart if it is not well cooled. This cake can be stored in an airtight container for up to 2 days.

CHOCOLATE CHARLOTTE

SERVES 10

1 torte pastry (see Basic Recipes on page 11)

2 tablespoons powdered sugar

2 cups heavy cream

1 1/2 cups bittersweet chocolate, chopped into small pieces

1 pound raspberries, preferably fresh but you may also use frozen

TOOLS

2 baking sheets

Parchment paper

Pastry bag with 1/4 -inch round tip

10-inch baking ring

Cellophane collar

Tangy fresh raspberries are the secret to this luscious chocolate dessert.

1. Preheat the oven to 350°F. Cover the baking sheets with parchment.

2. Fill the pastry bag with the torte pastry.

3. Using the pastry bag, pipe 2 circles of pastry, 10 inches in diameter, onto one of the baking sheets. Fill the circles from the outside moving inwards.

4. Still using the pastry bag, pipe 3-inch long strips of pastry onto the other baking sheet. Make two rows down the length of the pan or until you've used all the pastry, and space the strips 2 inches apart. Sprinkle powdered sugar on top.

5. Place the baking sheets in the oven for 15 minutes. Transfer the sheets to a cooling rack and let them cool for at least 30 minutes.

6. Prepare the ganache. Bring the cream to a boil in a small saucepan. Place the chocolate in a large mixing bowl. Remove the cream from the heat and pour it over the chocolate. Whisk until smooth. Set aside.

7. Turn the baked pastry over so that the parchment is facing upwards. Remove the parchment slowly and carefully so as not to break the pastry. (If the pastry breaks you can repair it later.)

8. Set the baking ring onto the baking sheet which will go into the freezer and line it with the cellophane collar. Place the baked pastry round carefully into the ring. Set the strips of pastry on the disc so that the strips are perpendicular to the round, vertically lining the edge of the pan.

9. Pour half the ganache into the baking ring and pour half the raspberries on top. Freeze for at least 30 minutes.

10. Remove the cake from the freezer and place the other pastry round on top. Pour the remaining ganache on top. Then pour the remaining raspberries over the cake. Freeze for another 30 minutes.

11. Remove the ring from the cake and wait 30 minutes before removing the cellophane collar and serving. This cake can be stored in the refrigerator for up to 2 days.

SERVES 10

1/2 pistachio torte pastry (see Basic Recipes on page 11)

2 cups heavy cream

1 cup bittersweet chocolate

1 tablespoon brandy

1/3 cup sugar

1/4 cup pistachios, coarsely crushed

TOOLS
2 baking sheets

Parchment paper

This roulade is perfect for a sophisticated palette.

1. Preheat the oven to 350°F.

2. Cover the baking sheets with parchment paper.

3. Pour half the torte pastry onto one of the baking sheets and spread it out with a spatula into a rectangle, 15 x 12 inches. Scatter half the pistachios over the pastry. Repeat with the remaining dough on the second baking sheet.

4. Bake for 12 minutes.

5. Remove the sheets from the oven and set them to cool on metal cooling racks for 1 hour.

6. Prepare the ganache. Bring 1 cup of the cream to a boil over a medium flame.

7. Place the chocolate in a large mixing bowl. Pour the boiling cream over the chocolate. Add the brandy to the melted chocolate and whisk until smooth. Set aside for 10 minutes.

8. After 10 minutes, put the mixture into the refrigerator for 30 minutes.

9. In a large mixing bowl, whip the remaining cream and sugar until soft peaks are formed.

10. Remove the ganache from the refrigerator and using a spatula, fold it into the whipped cream and combine the cream and chocolate until the mixture forms a smooth mousse.

11. Place the baked torte pastry onto a work surface with the side that was on the baking paper face up. With a spatula, spread a generous layer of mousse evenly on the pastry.

12. Carefully roll the pastry into a roulade and cover with plastic wrap. Freeze for at least 1 hour.

13. Take the roulade out of the freezer and remove the plastic wrap. Cut into 1/2-inch slices, arrange on plates, and wait 10 minutes before serving. This cake can be stored in an airtight container for up to 2 days.

CHOCOLATE FUDGE

SERVES 10

2 cups bittersweet chocolate

1 cup butter

6 eggs

2/3 cup of sugar

2 tablespoons quality coffee liqueur

1/2 cup flour

TOOLS
8 x 10-inch baking pan

Parchment paper

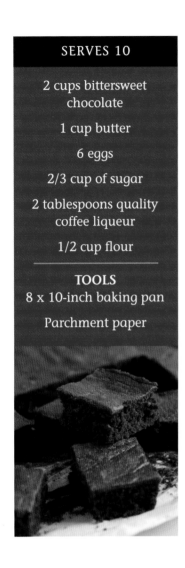

This recipe is easy to make and a treat to eat!

1. Preheat the oven to 350°F.

2. Melt the chocolate and butter in the top of a double boiler.

3. Beat together the eggs and the sugar with an electric mixer until foamy and well mixed.

4. When the chocolate and butter are completely melted, reduce the heat and mix in the coffee liqueur with a rubber spatula.

5. Fold the flour into the melted chocolate with a rubber spatula. Fold in the beaten egg mixture.

6. Line the baking pan with parchment paper and pour in the chocolate mixture.

7. Place the pan in the oven for 8 minutes.

8. Remove the pan and set to cool on a metal cooling rack for 30 minutes. Transfer to the refrigerator for at least 2 hours.

9. Remove the fudge from the refrigerator and transfer to a work surface. With a sharp knife, cut into 1-inch squares. Wipe the knife with a damp cloth between cuts to ensure clean edges.

10. Wait 20 minutes. Serve the fudge at room temperature. Fudge can be stored in an airtight container for up to 1 week.

CRISPY PECAN CHOCOLATE CAKE

SERVES 8

1 cup bittersweet
chocolate

1/2 cup butter

5 eggs

1 cup sugar

1 tablespoon Amaretto

1/3 cup flour

1 1/2 cups pecans,
coarsely crushed

Whipped cream (for
decoration)

TOOLS
10-inch springform
baking pan

You can replace the pecans with hazelnuts and create a totally different but equally delicious cake.

1. Preheat the oven to 350°F.

2. Melt the chocolate and the butter in the top of a double boiler.

3. Beat the eggs and sugar together with an electric mixer until frothy.

4. When the chocolate and butter are completely melted, remove from the heat and with a rubber spatula, mix in the Amaretto.

5. Fold the flour and the crushed pecans into the melted chocolate using a rubber spatula. Fold in the beaten egg mixture.

6. Pour the mixture into the springform pan and bake for 25 minutes. Remove from the oven and let it cool on a metal cooling rack for 30 minutes.

7. After the cake is cool, decorate with whipped cream or crème fraiche and serve immediately. This cake can be stored in an airtight container for up to 2 days.

WALNUT CHOCOLATE CRUNCH CAKE

Enjoy the great taste of chocolate and walnuts. You will love the added crunch!

1. Use an electric mixer on low speed to knead the yeast, water, egg, sugar, and flour in a large bowl for 3 minutes.

2. Add the salt and butter and continue to knead for another 5 minutes on medium speed.

3. Remove the dough from the mixing bowl and transfer to a floured bowl. Refrigerate for 1 hour.

4. Melt 1 cup of chocolate and the butter in the top of a double boiler.

5. When the chocolate and butter have completely melted, add cocoa and with an electric mixer, mix well until smooth. Set aside.

6. Remove the dough from the refrigerator and place on a floured work surface.

7. Roll out the dough into a 10 x 20-inch rectangle, 1/2-inch thick.

8. Wrap the chilled butter in baking paper and roll out the butter 1/4-inch thick. Unwrap the top of the butter and place the butter on the center of the dough. Remove the baking paper from the butter and fold up the four corners of the dough so that they meet and cover the butter.

9. Sprinkle a small amount of flour on the dough and roll out the dough to another 10 x 20-inch rectangle. Fold in the long sides of the rectangle to the middle and fold the new rectangle in half. Cover in plastic wrap and refrigerate for 30 minutes.

10. Remove the dough from the refrigerator and place on a floured work surface. Sprinkle a small amount of flour on the dough. Roll out the dough once more to 10 x 20-inch rectangle, 1/2-inch thick. Fold in the long sides of the rectangle and fold the new rectangle in half, as before.

11. Wrap the dough in plastic wrap and refrigerate for 30 minutes.

12. On a floured work surface, divide the dough into two equal halves. With a floured rolling pin, roll each section into a 5 x 12-inch rectangle, 1/8-inch thick. Spread half the filling on each rectangle and sprinkle half of the walnuts on top. Roll each rectangle into a roulade. Braid the two rolls together and crimp the ends to seal the braid.

13. Grease the pan and place the dough inside it. Brush the dough with the beaten egg and let the dough rise for 1 1/2 hours or until it triples in size.

Continued on page 52

14. Bake for 30 minutes or until the cake is browned.

15. Leave the cake to cool in the pan for 1 hour and then transfer to a metal cooling rack. Serve at room temperature. This cake can be stored in an airtight container for up to 3 days.

CHOCOLATE AMBROSIA

Ambrosia has two meanings: food of the gods and a 20th-century American dessert.

1. Preheat the oven to 350°F. Cover the baking sheets with parchment.

2. Fill the pastry bag with the torte pastry.

3. Pipe an 11-inch round of pastry onto a baking sheet starting from the outside and filling the round inwards. Bake for 15 minutes.

4. Remove from the oven and transfer the baked round to a metal cooling rack for at least 30 minutes.

5. Prepare the first mousse layer. Bring 1 cup of cream to a boil. When the cream boils, reduce the heat. Add 6 ounces of chocolate to the cream and whisk until smooth. Set aside.

6. Prepare the sugar syrup. Pour the water and sugar into a small saucepan and bring to a boil over a low flame. Do not stir the sugar while it is boiling. Set aside to cool at room temperature.

7. Turn the baked pastry over so that the parchment is facing upwards. Remove the parchment slowly and carefully so as not to break the pastry. (If the pastry breaks you can repair it later.) Set the pastry on a baking sheet with the side that was covered face-up.

8. Using the baking ring, cut a 10-inch circle of the dough.

9. Set the baking ring onto the baking sheet that will go into the freezer and line it with the cellophane collar. Place the baked pastry round carefully into the ring with the side that was covered facing up.

10. Pour the sugar syrup evenly over the cake. Spread the chocolate mousse on top. Smooth the surface of the mousse with a spatula. Freeze for 20 minutes.

11. Prepare the chocolate-almond mousse. Melt 6 ounces of chocolate and the marzipan in the top of a double boiler. In a medium mixing bowl, whip 1 cup of cream until it forms soft peaks. Fold the whipped cream into the chocolate and marzipan mixture using a rubber spatula until it forms a smooth, even mixture.

SERVES 10

1 cocoa torte pastry (see Basic Recipes on page 11)

3 cups heavy cream

18 ounces bittersweet chocolate, chopped

1/4 cup water

1/4 cup of sugar

4 ounces packaged marzipan

1/2 cup royal chocolate frosting (see Basic recipes on page 12)

TOOLS

2 baking sheets, one for baking and one for freezing

Parchment paper

Pastry bag with 1/4-inch round tip

10-inch baking ring

Cellophane collar

---

12. Remove the cake from the freezer and spread the chocolate-almond mousse evenly over the cake using a frosting knife. Return the cake to the freezer for 20 minutes.

13. Prepare the chocolate mousse. Melt the remaining 6 ounces of chocolate in a double boiler. Whip the remaining cream until it forms soft peaks, and fold it into the chocolate with a rubber spatula until the mixture is smooth.

14. Remove the cake from the freezer and spread the third layer of mousse on the cake evenly with a frosting knife, taking care that the mousse touches the edges of the cellophane collar. Return the cake to the freezer until it is completely frozen. At this stage, you can store the cake in the freezer for up to 2 weeks.

15. Remove the cake from the freezer. Using a frosting knife, spread a generous layer of royal chocolate frosting on the top and sides of the frozen cake. Spread the frosting carefully as the frosting has a tendency to harden when it comes into contact with the frozen cake. Place the cake in the refrigerator to defrost. Remove the baking ring and the plastic collar and serve. You may store the cake in the refrigerator for up to 3 days.

BANANA CHOCOLATE CAKE

SERVES 8

1 tablespoon butter to grease the pan

1 1/2 cups bittersweet chocolate

1 cup butter

6 eggs

2/3 cup sugar

1 tablespoon banana liqueur

1/2 cup flour

3 large ripe bananas, cut into 1/4-inch pieces

TOOLS
10-inch springform baking pan

This light and tasty cake is easy to make and impressive to serve.

1. Preheat the oven to 325°F and lightly grease the springform pan with butter.

2. Melt the chocolate and butter in the top of a double boiler.

3. While the chocolate is melting, use an electric mixer to beat the eggs and sugar together until stiff.

4. When the chocolate is melted, remove from the heat. Add the banana liqueur and mix with a rubber spatula.

5. Fold the flour into the chocolate and mix well. Fold in the bananas. When the mixture is combined well, fold in the eggs.

6. Pour the mixture into the springform pan.

7. Bake for 25 minutes or until a toothpick inserted into the center comes out clean.

8. When the cake is done, let it cool on a wire rack for 30 minutes.

9. This cake is delicious served warm and can be stored in the refrigerator for up to 2 days.

CHOCOLATE MUFFINS

Warm chocolate muffins are perfect to accompany your morning cup of coffee or as an afternoon snack.

1. Preheat the oven to 375°F.

2. Combine the milk and butter in a small saucepan, bring to just below boiling, and then remove from the heat.

3. While the milk is boiling, in a large bowl, stir together the dry ingredients using a wooden spoon. Pour the milk and butter mixture into the bowl, add the egg, and stir well until the mixture is smooth and uniform.

4. Add the chopped chocolate and mix well. Set aside for 15 minutes. At this stage, you can store the mixture in the refrigerator for up to 24 hours.

5. Grease the muffin tin and spoon the mixture into each cup until it is 3/4 full.

6. Bake for 18-20 minutes or until the muffins are golden brown and a toothpick inserted in the middle comes out clean. If necessary, rotate the muffin tin in the oven so that the muffins brown evenly.

7. When the muffins are baked, remove them from the muffin tin while they are still warm and transfer them to a metal cooling rack.

8. For best results, serve the muffins while they are fresh and warm. However, you can store them and serve them up to several hours later.

CHOCOLATE HAZELNUT BROWNIES

MAKES APPROXIMATELY 20 BROWNIES

1 1/2 cups bittersweet chocolate

1 cup butter

5 eggs

3/4 cup sugar

3/4 cup hazelnuts, whole

1/2 cup flour

TOOLS

8 x 10-inch baking pan

Parchment paper

Moist and delicious brownies with a delightful nutty crunch.

1. Preheat the oven to 350°F.

2. Melt the chocolate and butter in the top of a double boiler.

3. While the chocolate is melting, beat the eggs and sugar together with an electric mixer until they are frothy.

4. When the chocolate and butter are completely melted, remove from the heat and stir in the hazelnuts with a rubber spatula.

5. Fold the flour into the melted chocolate with a spatula. Fold the beaten eggs into the mixture.

6. Line the baking pan with parchment paper. Pour the mixture into the baking pan and bake at 350°F for 8 minutes.

7. Remove the pan from the oven and set to cool on a metal cooling rack for 30 minutes. After 30 minutes, transfer to the refrigerator for at least 2 hours.

8. After the brownies cool, remove from the refrigerator and set on a work surface. Cut the brownies into 2-inch squares with a sharp knife. Be sure to wipe the knife with a damp cloth between cuts to ensure clean lines.

9. Serve at room temperature. The brownies can be stored in an airtight container for up to 3 days.

GANACHE-FILLED BRIOCHE

Brioche is a roll or bun made from yeast dough. This brioche is filled with succulent chocolate cream.

1. Using the kneading hook, mix the eggs, milk, yeast, sugar, and the flour with an electric mixer on a low speed for 3 minutes. While the mixer is running, add the salt. Increase the mixing speed to medium and continue to mix for 7 more minutes. Gradually add the butter and continue to mix for 3 minutes until the mixture forms a uniform, smooth dough.

2. Cover the mixing bowl with plastic wrap and refrigerate overnight.

3. Place the cream in a small saucepan and bring to a boil over a medium flame. While the cream is boiling, place the chocolate in a large bowl. When the cream has boiled, pour the cream over the chocolate to melt. Whisk the chocolate and cream until they are smooth and thick.

4. Freeze the chocolate cream for 30 minutes.

5. When the cream has solidified somewhat, remove from the freezer. Grease your fingers with a small amount of oil. Using your hands, scoop out a ball of cream around the size of a heaping teaspoonful. Roll the chocolate cream into a 1-inch round ball. Set the ball on the plastic wrap covered plate. Repeat with the rest of the cream and store in the refrigerator.

6. Transfer the chilled dough to a floured work surface and flatten it with your hand to remove any air pockets. Divide the dough into three equal parts. Divide each part into four quarters. Roll each section of dough into a ball. You will have 12 balls of dough.

7. Press your finger into each ball and create a small indentation. Remove the chilled balls of chocolate cream from the refrigerator. Carefully place a ball of cream in each ball of dough so that the cream is even with the dough. Set the dough ball in a double greased brioche mold. Repeat with each ball of dough. Place all the molds on a baking sheet, 1-inch apart. Brush each ball of dough with the beaten egg.

8. Allow the dough to rise at room temperature for 2 hours or until it has tripled in size.

9. Bake in an oven that has been preheated to 375°F for 15 minutes or until golden brown.

10. Serve immediately and do not store.

Note: The dough must remain chilled when forming the brioche. If the dough becomes warmed while working with it, wrap it in plastic wrap and chill in the freezer until it solidifies again.

CHOCOLATE RUGELACH

MAKES 60

FOR THE DOUGH
2 tablespoons fresh yeast

1/2 cup water

1 egg

3 tablespoons sugar

2 1/2cups flour

1 teaspoon salt

1/4 cup butter, softened

FOR THE FILLING
1 cup bittersweet chocolate

1/2 cup butter

1/4 cup premium cocoa

1/2 cup chilled butter for folding

1 egg, beaten

Syrup of 3/4 cup boiling water mixed with 1 cup sugar

TOOLS
Electric mixer with kneading hook

Baking paper

Rolling pin

2 baking sheets

Gourmet recipe for the classic Jewish delicacy.

1. Place the yeast, water, egg, sugar, and flour in the mixing bowl. Mix on a low speed with the kneading hook for 3 minutes.

2. Add the salt and butter and increase the mixing speed to medium and continue to mix for 5 minutes.

3. Remove the dough from the mixer and transfer to a floured bowl. Cover with plastic wrap and refrigerate for 1 hour.

4. Prepare the filling. Melt the chocolate and butter in the top of a double boiler.

5. When the chocolate and butter are melted, add the cocoa and whisk until smooth and uniform. Store at room temperature for later.

6. Remove the dough from the refrigerator and transfer to a floured work surface.

7. Roll out the dough to form a 10 x 20-inch rectangle, 1/2-inch thick.

8. Wrap the chilled butter in baking paper and roll out to 1/4-inch thick. Remove the baking paper from the top of the butter and turn the butter onto the rolled-out dough. Remove the rest of the baking paper and fold the four sides of the dough inwards to cover the butter.

9. Sprinkle flour on the dough and roll out again to the same dimensions as before. Fold the long sides of the dough inwards to the center and then fold the new rectangle in half. Wrap in plastic wrap and refrigerate for 30 minutes.

10. Remove the dough from the refrigerator and transfer to a floured work surface. Sprinkle a small amount of flour on the dough. Roll out the dough to form a 10 x 20-inch rectangle, 1/2-inch thick. Fold in the long sides and fold in half again.

11. Wrap the dough in plastic wrap and refrigerate for 1 hour.

12. Transfer to a floured work surface. Divide the dough into two equal portions. Roll out each portion with a floured rolling pin. Roll out each portion to form a 5 x 12-inch rectangle, 1/8th-inch thick. Spread 1/4 of the filling on each portion and fold in half. Roll out the dough again and spread half the remaining filling on each portion. Fold the dough in half again and roll out as thin as possible.

13. With a sharp knife cut out isosceles triangles that are 2 inches in length. Roll each triangle lengthwise from the base to the tip like a

Continued on page 66

croissant. Place the rugelach on a baking sheet 1/2-inch apart. Brush each one with beaten egg.

14. Set the baking sheets in a warm place for 40 minutes. Bake for 15 minutes in an oven that has been preheated to 375°F. Bake 30 rugelach at a time.

15. Remove the rugelach from the oven and generously brush each one with the sugar syrup using the pastry brush. Allow to cool for 30 minutes before serving. You can store the rugelach in an airtight container for up to 2 days.

CHOCOLATE TUILE COOKIES

MAKES 20

1/4 cup freshly squeezed orange juice

2 egg whites

1/2 cup powdered sugar

2/3 cup melted butter

1 tablespoon flour

1 tablespoon cocoa

1/4 cup bittersweet chocolate, grated

1/4 cup bleached almonds, ground

TOOLS
Baking sheet covered with silicone sheet

These delicate chocolate cookies can be filled or eaten plain.

1. Preheat the oven to 350°F.

2. In a large bowl, whisk together the orange juice, egg whites, powdered sugar, and melted butter. Whisk until smooth.

3. Add the flour, cocoa, and chocolate and mix well. Add the bleached almonds and mix until the mixture is uniform.

4. Place generous spoonfuls of the mixture on the baking sheet 3 inches apart. Flatten each spoonful with the back of a spoon to form 2-inch rounds. Bake in batches of five cookies.

5. Bake for 10 minutes or until the center of each cookie is dry.

6. Remove from the oven and, using a thick spatula, remove each cookie from the baking sheet. Carefully bend each cookie around a rolling pin to form an arched shape. If the cookies are too brittle to bend, return them to the oven for a few seconds.

7. Let the cookies cool for 10 minutes on the rolling pin and carefully transfer them to an airtight storage container.

8. Best served within 12 hours.

CHOCOLATE MARBLE COOKIES

**MAKES
APPROXIMATELY
30 COOKIES**

1/2 cup chilled butter

1/4 cup powdered sugar

2 eggs

1/2 cup water

1/2 teaspoon salt

2 cups flour

1 tablespoon premium
cocoa

TOOLS
Food processor

2 baking sheets

Rolling pin

Pastry brush

These beautiful cookies are as delicious as they are attractive.

1. Preheat the oven to 375°F.

2. Place the butter and powdered sugar in the food processor and process for 2 minutes or until the mixture is smooth.

3. Turn off the processor and add 1 egg, water, salt, and half the flour. Process for 2 more minutes until the dough is smooth and uniform. Add the rest of the flour and continue to process for 1 minute or until the dough forms a ball.

4. Remove the ball of dough from the processor and transfer to a floured work surface. Divide the dough into two equal portions. Wrap one half in plastic wrap and refrigerate. Take the remaining half and knead the cocoa into the dough with your hands until the dough becomes dark brown. Wrap the chocolate dough in plastic wrap and refrigerate. Both wrapped portions should be refrigerated for at least 30 minutes.

5. Once the dough is chilled, transfer the white dough to a floured work surface and roll out the dough until it is 1/8-inch thick. Set aside. Transfer the chocolate dough to the work surface and roll it out until it is also 1/8-inch thick. Using a pastry brush, brush the top surface of the chocolate dough with water and place the white dough securely on top. Roll the two layers of dough together so that they form a long cylinder. With a sharp knife, slice the cylinder into 1/4-inch thick slices. Place the slices on the baking sheet 1/2-inch apart. There should be approximately 15 cookies per sheet.

6. Beat the remaining egg and using the pastry brush, brush each cookie with the beaten egg. Bake at 375°F for 15 minutes or until the white portion of the dough is golden brown.

7. When the cookies are baked, remove them from the baking sheet and place on a metal cooling rack for 30 minutes.

8. You may serve them immediately or store them in an airtight container for up to 1 week.

CHOCOLATE TUILE CONES

MAKES 20

20 tuile cookies baked, but not rolled (see Chocolate Tuile Cookies, page 66)

8 ounces bittersweet chocolate

1 1/2 cups heavy cream

1/3 cup sugar

1 tablespoon brandy

1/3 cup roasted cacao beans, coarsely ground

TOOLS

Pastry bag with 1/8th-inch flowered tip

Baking sheet

This wonderful confection will make a huge hit at any dinner party.

1. Prepare the tuile cookies until they are baking.

2. Remove from the oven and transfer each cookie to the baking sheet.

3. Using an oven mitt, form each cookie into a cone like an ice cream cone. Place the cones on a work surface so the seam is facing down and let them cool for 10 minutes. Prepare the cones in batches of five so you have time to form the cones before the cookies cool and become too brittle to work with.

4. Melt the chocolate in the top of a double boiler.

5. While the chocolate is melting, whip the cream and sugar with an electric mixer until they form soft peaks.

6. After the chocolate has melted, add the brandy and mix well.

7. Pour the chocolate into the cream and whisk by hand until smooth. Refrigerate the mixture for 20 minutes.

8. Place the chocolate mixture in the pastry bag and, using the flowered tip, fill each cone 3/4 full. Sprinkle the ground cacao beans on the filling. Refrigerate for at least 1 hour.

9. Serve the cones cold. You can store them in the refrigerator for up to 2 days.

DESSERTS

4

CHOCOLATE FONDUE

Chocolate fondue is a perfect accompaniment to all the lovely fresh fruits that are in abundance during the summer months.

1. Place the cream, chocolate, and orange zest in the fondue pot and heat over a low flame. Mix well using a hand whisk until the mixture is smooth and uniform.

2. Transfer the fondue pot to its base and light a candle underneath to keep the fondue warm.

3. Cut the bananas into 1-inch slices. Cut the oranges into 1-inch cubes. Remove the stems from the strawberries and leave them whole.

4. Arrange the fruit and the fondue forks on a large serving plate.

5. Serve immediately.

Variations:

*   You can replace the orange zest with 1/4-teaspoon of the following spices: ground cinnamon, nutmeg, and ground cloves.

*   Coffee lovers can replace the orange zest with 1 demitasse cup of espresso or 1 tablespoon of coffee liqueur.

*   You may also serve with other foods such as kiwi, pineapple, melon, chunks of cookies, tea biscuits, and marshmallows.

CHOCOLATE CRÈME BRÛLÉE

MAKES 6

2 cups heavy cream

2/3 cup sugar

5 ounces bittersweet chocolate

6 egg yolks

6 tablespoons brown sugar

TOOLS
6 small heat-proof ramekins or custard cups

2 baking pans with high sides

This classic restaurant dessert is easy to recreate at home. Wow your guests with this wonderfully sweet and creamy treat.

1. Preheat oven to 325°F.

2. In a small saucepan, combine the cream and the sugar and bring to a boil over a medium flame.

3. When the cream has boiled, place the chocolate in a large bowl and pour the cream over the chocolate to melt it. Whisk well until the mixture is smooth and uniform.

4. Add the egg yolks and whisk well until smooth.

5. Pour the mixture into the ramekins or custard cups and arrange them on the two baking pans.

6. Pour boiling water into the baking pans until it reaches halfway up the sides of the pans and bake for 20 minutes at 325°F.

7. Remove the pans from the oven and remove the cups from the pans. Let the custard cool at room temperature for 30 minutes.

8. Cover the cups with plastic wrap and refrigerate for 2 hours. At this stage, you may store the custard in the refrigerator for up to 3 days.

9. To serve, spread an even layer of brown sugar on each cup and place in the oven under the broiler for 1 minute to form a caramel crust. Serve immediately.

CHOCOLATE BREAD AND BUTTER PUDDING

SERVES 8

4 eggs, separated

1 cup sugar

2 cups whole milk

1/2 cup breadcrumbs

5 ounces bittersweet chocolate, chopped

TOOLS
Electric mixer

Bread and butter pudding is a traditional dessert popular in British cuisine.

1. Preheat the oven to 300°F. Place the egg whites in the mixer bowl and whip them until they form soft peaks. Gradually add half of the sugar and continue to whip until the mixture forms stiff peaks.

2. Place the egg yolks in a bowl with the remaining sugar and whisk them until they are mixed well.

3. Add the milk, breadcrumbs, and chocolate to the egg yolks and mix well until the mixture is smooth and uniform.

4. Fold the whipped egg whites into the mixture and mix well with a rubber spatula until the mixture is smooth and uniform.

5. Transfer the mixture to a large pan. The varying densities of the ingredients will cause them to separate into layers. The chocolate, being the heaviest, will sink in the bottom, while the breadcrumbs and the egg will rise to the top. Bake for 25 minutes. Remove from the oven and serve immediately.

See picture on opposite page.

INDIVIDUAL CHOCOLATE SOUFFLÉS

MAKES 6

3 eggs, separated

1/2 cup sugar

5 ounces bittersweet chocolate

1/2 cup butter

1 tablespoon cocoa

2 tablespoons flour

1/3 cup powdered sugar (for decoration)

TOOLS
6-cup muffin tin

This luxurious recipe is easy to make and will soon become a favorite in your home.

1. Preheat the oven to 375°F and grease the muffin tin.

2. In a large bowl, use an electric hand mixer to whip the egg whites with 1/4 cup of sugar until they form stiff peaks.

3. In a separate bowl, beat the egg yolks with the remaining sugar until the mixture is airy and smooth.

4. Melt the chocolate, butter, and cocoa in the top of a double boiler.

5. Combine the whipped egg whites, beaten yolks, and chocolate mixture using a rubber spatula. When the three mixtures are combined, gradually fold in the flour.

6. Pour the finished soufflé batter in equal amounts into each muffin cup. Bake for 12 minutes.

7. Use a small spoon to gently and carefully remove each soufflé from the muffin tin. To serve, sprinkle powdered sugar on each soufflé and serve immediately.

CHOCOLATE PROFITEROLES

Elegant pastries filled with succulent chocolate cream are the perfect showcase dessert for impressing your dinner guests.

1. Preheat the oven to 375°F.

2. In a small saucepan, combine the water, milk, butter, sugar, and salt, and bring to a boil over a medium flame.

3. Add the flour and simmer over a low flame while stirring until the dough forms a ball.

4. Chill the dough slightly by transferring the dough to an electric mixer and mixing for 3 minutes on a low speed.

5. Add 4 eggs to the dough. Add each egg separately and be sure that each egg is completely mixed into the dough before adding the next egg.

6. Cover the mixing bowl with plastic wrap and refrigerate for at least 30 minutes. You may store the wrapped dough in the refrigerator for up to 24 hours.

7. Transfer the dough to a pastry bag and attach the 1/2-inch round tip.

8. Pipe 1-inch rounds of dough onto the baking sheet 1-inch apart. Beat the remaining egg and brush each round with egg using a pastry brush. Bake for 25 minutes at 375°F.

9. While the profiteroles are baking, prepare the filling. In a small saucepan bring 1/2 a cup of cream to a boil over a medium flame.

10. Place the chocolate in a large bowl and pour the boiling cream over the chocolate to melt. Whisk well until the mixture is smooth and uniform.

11. Whip the remaining cream and sugar until it forms soft peaks. Fold in the chocolate using a rubber spatula. Set aside in the refrigerator.

12. Remove the profiteroles from the oven and transfer to a cooling rack for 20 minutes.

13. Prepare the sauce while the profiteroles are cooling. Heat the cream in a small saucepan over a medium flame and bring to a boil. Remove from the heat and add the chocolate. Whisk well until the chocolate is melted. Set aside.

14. Place the chocolate cream inside the pastry bag and attach the 1/4-inch round tip. Pipe into each pastry a generous amount of cream. Refrigerate the filled pastries for at least 1 hour. At this stage, you may store the filled pastries another 2 days in the refrigerator.

Continued on page 80

15. Remove the profiteroles from the refrigerator and arrange them on a serving plate. Pour a generous amount of chocolate sauce over the pastries.

16. Serve immediately.

RICH CHOCOLATE ICE CREAM

SERVES 6

1/2 cup whole milk

1/2 cup heavy cream

1 vanilla bean

3/4 cup sugar

4 egg yolks

5 ounces bittersweet chocolate

1 tablespoon brandy

TOOLS
Candy thermometer

Fine mesh sieve

Ice cream maker

There's nothing more refreshing than a scoop of chocolate ice cream on a hot summer's day.

1. Place the milk, cream, vanilla bean, and half the sugar into a saucepan and bring to a boil over a medium flame.

2. Place the egg yolks and the remaining sugar in a bowl and whisk well until smooth and uniform.

3. When the milk mixture boils, reduce the heat and carefully pour the egg yolks into the mixture.

4. With a wooden spoon, stir the mixture in the saucepan as it cooks, and when it reaches 175°F remove the mixture from the heat.

5. Pour the mixture through a fine sieve into a large bowl to achieve a smooth liquid with no lumps.

6. Quickly add the chocolate and mix well until all the chocolate is melted.

7. When the chocolate is melted, add the brandy and mix well.

8. Cover the bowl with plastic wrap and allow it to cool slightly. After the mixture cools, refrigerate for at least 4 hours so that the liquid becomes very chilled.

9. Pour the liquid into the ice cream maker and turn on the machine. Process the ice cream until it achieves the desired texture.

STEAMED CHOCOLATE PUDDING

SERVES 6

6 ounces bittersweet chocolate

3/4 cup butter

3 eggs

3 egg yolks

1/2 cup sugar

1 tablespoon brandy

2 tablespoons flour

TO SERVE
Whipped cream or vanilla ice cream

TOOLS
6 silicone individual size tube pans or non–stick Teflon pans

Baking pan with high sides

A dessert for a cold rainy night is something you must have in your cooking repertoire.

1. Preheat the oven to 275°F.

2. Melt the chocolate and butter in the top of a double boiler.

3. Beat the eggs, yolks, and sugar until they are foamy.

4. Add the melted chocolate and brandy to the eggs and mix well.

5. Fold in the flour with a rubber spatula.

6. Divide the mixture between the six small pans and place them in the baking pan. Pour hot water inside the pan until it reaches halfway up the sides of the tube pans.

7. Bake for 45 minutes at 275°F.

8. Remove from the oven and let cool for 30 minutes in a well-ventilated area, such as near a window.

9. Serve immediately with whipped cream or vanilla ice cream.

STRAWBERRY CHOCOLATE NAPOLEONS

A delightful variation of classic napoleons arranged with fresh strawberries.

FOR THE CHOCOLATE TUILE PASTRY

1/4 cup freshly squeezed orange juice

2 egg whites

1/2 cup powdered sugar

2/3 cup melted butter

1 tablespoon flour

1 tablespoon cocoa

1/4 cup bittersweet chocolate, grated

1/4 cup bleached almonds, ground

FOR THE CREAM

2 cups heavy cream

5 ounces bittersweet chocolate

1/3 cup sugar

30 fresh whole strawberries

TOOLS

Baking sheet covered with silicone baking sheet

Pastry bag with 1/4-inch round tip

1. Preheat the oven to 350°F.

2. In a large bowl, combine the orange juice, egg whites, powdered sugar, and melted butter. Whisk well until smooth and uniform.

3. Add the flour, cocoa, and chocolate and mix well. Add the almonds and continue to mix until smooth and uniform.

4. Place heaping spoonfuls of the mixture on the baking sheet 3 inches apart. Flatten each spoonful with the back of the spoon to form 2-inch rounds. Bake in two batches of 6.

5. Bake for 10 minutes until the center of each round is dry.

6. Remove from the oven and let cool for 30 minutes.

7. While the tuiles are cooling, bring 1/2 cup of cream to a boil over a medium flame.

8. Place the chocolate in a large bowl and pour the boiling cream over it to melt the chocolate. Whisk until the mixture is smooth and uniform.

9. Whip the remaining cream with the sugar using an electric mixer until it forms stiff peaks. Fold the chocolate into the whipped cream using a rubber spatula. Transfer the chocolate cream to the pastry bag with the 1/4-inch tip.

10. To assemble the napoleons, place one tuile pastry on a plate, pipe a generous layer of cream in the center, and arrange strawberries around the sides. Place another tuile pastry on top at a 45° angle. Serve immediately.

CHOCOLATE PAVLOVA WITH CITRUS MOUSSE

Crispy chocolate meringue filled with luscious citrus-accented chocolate mousse.

SERVES 8

6 egg whites

1 1/2 cups sugar

1 tablespoon balsamic vinegar

3 tablespoons cocoa

1/4 cup bittersweet chocolate, finely grated

FOR THE MOUSSE
2 cups heavy cream

5 ounces bittersweet chocolate

1 tablespoon citrus liqueur

1/3 cup sugar

Zest of 1 whole orange

TOOLS
Baking sheet covered with parchment paper

Electric mixer

1. Place the egg whites in the bowl of the electric mixer and beat them until they form soft peaks. Gradually add the sugar and continue to beat the egg whites until they form stiff peaks.

2. Remove the bowl from the mixer. Fold in the vinegar, cocoa, and chocolate using a spatula.

3. Preheat the oven to 375°F.

4. Spoon 3-inch rounds of the chocolate meringue mixture 1/2-inch apart onto the baking paper and press down gently in the center of each round with a spoon to create an impression.

5. Bake for 5 minutes.

6. Reduce the oven temperature to 300°F and bake for another hour and 15 minutes.

7. While the meringue is baking, prepare the filling. In a small saucepan, bring 1/2 a cup of cream to a boil over a medium flame.

8. Place the chocolate in a large bowl and pour the boiling cream over the chocolate to melt it. Whisk well until smooth. Add the liqueur and mix well.

9. Whip the remaining cream with the sugar until it forms stiff peaks. Add the orange zest. Fold in the chocolate mixture with a spatula and mix well. Refrigerate for 30 minutes.

10. Remove the pavlovas from the oven and let cool on a cooling rack for 30 minutes.

11. Carefully remove the pavlovas from the baking paper and set them on serving plates. Place a generous amount of mousse in the center of each and serve.

Note: You may serve this as a single, family-sized portion by preparing the pavlova as a single large heap of meringue. To serve, place the pavlova in the center of a serving tray and fill with the mousse.

5

PRALINES
AND
TRUFFLES

PISTACHIO CREAM PRALINES

MAKES 50

1/2 cup shelled pistachios

1/2 cup heavy cream

12 ounces bittersweet chocolate

9 ounces white chocolate

TOOLS
Food processor with rounded blade

Candy thermometer

Praline moulds

Pastry bag with 1/3-inch round tip

Pralines were originally called "prasline" and were named after the French diplomat Marshal du Plessis-Praslin, whose cook supposedly invented them.

1. In the food processor, mix the pistachios and the cream. Process until smooth. Set aside.

2. Melt the bittersweet chocolate in the top of a double boiler.

3. After the chocolate has melted, transfer to a bowl and whisk by hand in a well-ventilated place, such as next to a window.

4. Let the chocolate cool to room temperature. Monitor the temperature of the chocolate by measuring it every 5 minutes with the thermometer. Let the chocolate cool to 86°F. Be patient, because if the chocolate does not cool properly the pralines will be chalky and not glossy.

5. While the chocolate is cooling, melt the white chocolate in the top of a double boiler. When the white chocolate is completely melted, add the pistachio cream mixture to the double boiler. Mix well until the mixture is completely blended and is of uniform texture.

6. When the bittersweet chocolate has cooled, whisk until the chocolate achieves a smooth glossy texture. Generously ladle the melted bittersweet chocolate into the praline moulds. Fill the moulds completely. Turn the mould over onto a bowl and drain the moulds of chocolate so that only a coating of chocolate remains in each mould. Freeze the pralines for 5 minutes.

7. Place the white chocolate mixture in the pastry bag with the round tip. Remove the praline moulds from the freezer and pipe the white chocolate mixture into each praline until it is just below the edge of the mould. Freeze for 15 minutes.

8. Remove the pralines from the freezer and ladle a layer of bittersweet chocolate over the pralines. Spread the chocolate evenly with a rubber spatula or a pastry knife so that it does not overflow from the individual moulds. Freeze for 30 minutes.

9. Remove the pralines from the freezer, turn the moulds over, and hold them 2 inches above your work surface. Slap the bottom of the mould with your hand to free the pralines from their moulds.

10. Serve immediately or transfer to an airtight container and store in a cool dark place for up to 2 weeks.

See picture of assorted pralines on opposite page.

DULCE DE LECHE PRALINES

MAKES 30

12 ounces quality
bittersweet chocolate

1 cup quality dulche de
leche

TOOLS
Candy thermometer

Pastry bag with 1/3-inch
round tip

Praline moulds

If you cannot find dulce de leche, you may use a good quality caramel spread instead.

1. Melt the chocolate in the top of a double boiler.

2. After the chocolate has melted, transfer to a bowl and whisk by hand for 1 minute in a well-ventilated place, such as next to a window.

3. Let the chocolate cool to room temperature. Monitor the temperature of the chocolate by measuring it every 5 minutes with the thermometer. Let the chocolate cool to 86°F. Be patient, because if the chocolate does not cool properly the pralines will be chalky and not glossy.

4. When the chocolate has cooled, whisk until the chocolate achieves a smooth glossy texture. Generously ladle the melted chocolate into the praline moulds. Fill the moulds completely. Turn the mould over onto a bowl and drain the moulds of chocolate so that only a coating of chocolate remains in each mould. Freeze the pralines for 5 minutes.

5. Place the dulche de leche in the pastry bag with the round tip. Remove the praline moulds from the freezer and pipe the dulche de leche into each praline until it is just below the edge of the mould. Freeze for 15 minutes.

6. Remove the pralines from the freezer and ladle a layer of bittersweet chocolate over the pralines. Spread the chocolate evenly with a rubber spatula or a pastry knife so that it does not overflow from the individual moulds. Freeze for 30 minutes.

7. Remove the pralines from the freezer, turn the moulds over, and hold them 2 inches above your work surface. Slap the bottom of the mould with your hand to free the pralines from their moulds.

8. Serve immediately or transfer to an airtight container and store in a cool dark place for up to 2 weeks.

NOUGAT PRALINES

MAKES 30

12 ounces bittersweet chocolate

Nougatine, puréed (see Basic Recipes on page 13)

TOOLS
Candy thermometer

Praline moulds

Pastry bag with 1/3-inch round tip

The Italian word for nougat is "torrone". It is named after a type of ancient tower called a "torrazzo".

1. Melt the chocolate in the top of a double boiler.

2. After the chocolate has melted, transfer to a bowl and whisk by hand for 1 minute in a well-ventilated place, such as next to a window.

3. Let the chocolate cool to room temperature. Monitor the temperature of the chocolate by measuring it every 5 minutes with the thermometer. Let the chocolate cool to 86°F. Be patient, because if the chocolate does not cool properly the pralines will be chalky and not glossy.

4. When the chocolate has cooled, whisk until the chocolate achieves a smooth glossy texture. Generously ladle the melted chocolate into the praline moulds. Fill the moulds completely. Turn the mould over onto a bowl and drain the moulds of chocolate so that only a coating of chocolate remains in each mould. Freeze the pralines for 5 minutes.

5. Place the nougat mixture in the pastry bag with the round tip. Remove the praline moulds from the freezer and pipe the nougat mixture into each praline until it is just below the edge of the mould. Freeze for 15 minutes.

6. Remove the pralines from the freezer and ladle a layer of bittersweet chocolate over the pralines. Spread the chocolate evenly with a rubber spatula or a pastry knife so that it does not overflow from the individual moulds. Freeze for 30 minutes.

7. Remove the pralines from the freezer, turn the moulds over, and hold them 2 inches above your work surface. Slap the bottom of the mould with your hand to free the pralines from their moulds.

8. Serve immediately or transfer to an airtight container and store in a cool dark place for up to 2 weeks.

MOCHA CREAM PRALINES

Coffee and chocolate are two flavors which complement each other extremely well and are frequently combined.

1. In a small saucepan, bring the cream to a boil over a medium flame.

2. While the cream is boiling, place 6 ounces of chocolate in a bowl. When the cream has boiled, pour it over the chocolate and lightly whisk the mixture to combine. Add the coffee and mix well until the mixture is smooth and uniform. Refrigerate for 40 minutes.

3. While the coffee cream mixture is cooling, melt the remaining chocolate in the top of a double boiler.

4. After the chocolate has melted, transfer to a bowl and whisk by hand for one minute in a well-ventilated place, such as next to a window.

5. Let the chocolate cool to room temperature. Monitor the temperature of the chocolate by measuring it every 5 minutes with the thermometer. Let the chocolate cool to 86°F. Be patient, because if the chocolate does not cool properly the pralines will be chalky and not glossy.

6. When the bittersweet chocolate has cooled, whisk until the chocolate achieves a smooth glossy texture. Generously ladle the melted bittersweet chocolate into the praline moulds. Fill the moulds completely. Turn the mould over onto a bowl and drain the moulds of chocolate so that only a coating of chocolate remains in each mould. Freeze the pralines for 5 minutes.

7. Place the coffee cream mixture in the pastry bag with the round tip. Remove the praline moulds from the freezer and pipe the coffee cream mixture into each praline until it is just below the edge of the mould. Freeze for 15 minutes.

8. Remove the pralines from the freezer and ladle a layer of bittersweet chocolate over the pralines. Spread the chocolate evenly with a rubber spatula or a pastry knife so that it does not overflow from the individual moulds. Freeze for 30 minutes.

9. Remove the pralines from the freezer, turn the moulds over, and hold them 2 inches above your work surface. Slap the bottom of the mould with your hand to free the pralines from their moulds.

10. Serve immediately or transfer to an airtight container and store in a cool dark place up to 2 weeks.

BITTERSWEET CHOCOLATE TRUFFLES

MAKES 30

1 cup heavy cream

10 ounces bittersweet chocolate

1/2 cup premium cocoa

TOOLS

Pastry bag with 1/2-inch round tip

Disposable gloves

Baking paper

Baking sheet

This is the basic truffle recipe. Once you master this recipe, you can use your imagination to create a multitude of confectionary delights.

1. In a small saucepan, bring the cream to a boil over a medium flame.

2. Place the chocolate in a large bowl and pour the boiling cream over the chocolate to melt it. Whisk until smooth and uniform. Refrigerate for 30 minutes.

3. When the chocolate has cooled, transfer to the pastry bag. Pipe 1-inch rounds onto the baking paper 1/2-inch apart.

4. While wearing gloves, roll each round into a ball using the palm of your hands. Roll each ball in cocoa so that it is completely coated.

5. Place each ball on a baking sheet 1/2-inch apart. Let cool for one hour at room temperature until the chocolate hardens.

6. Serve immediately or store in an airtight container in a cool dark place for up to 2 weeks.

See picture on opposite page.

ESPRESSO CHOCOLATE TRUFFLES

MAKES 30

1 cup heavy cream

10 ounces bittersweet chocolate

1/4 cup espresso

1/4 cup powdered instant coffee

TOOLS

Pastry bag with 1/2-inch round tip

Whisk

Disposable gloves

Baking paper

Baking sheet

Another wonderful confection that combines the tastes of chocolate and coffee.

1. In a small saucepan, bring the cream to a boil over a medium flame.

2. Place the chocolate in a large bowl and pour the boiling cream over the chocolate to melt it. Add the espresso and whisk until smooth and uniform. Refrigerate for 30 minutes.

3. When the chocolate has cooled, transfer to the pastry bag. Pipe 1-inch rounds onto the baking paper 1/2-inch apart.

4. While wearing gloves, roll each round into a ball using the palms of your hands.

5. Roll each ball in the powdered coffee so that it is completely coated.

6. Place each ball on a baking sheet 1/2-inch apart. Let cool for 1 hour at room temperature until the chocolate hardens.

7. Serve immediately or store in an airtight container in a cool, dark place for up to 2 weeks.

CRISPY CHOCOLATE WALNUT FINGERS

Delightfully crunchy and chewy candies with a hint of almond liqueur to give them sophistication.

MAKES 32

1 1/2 cups heavy cream

14 ounces bittersweet chocolate

1 teaspoon Amaretto liqueur

Muscadine (see Basic Recipes on page 13)

TOOLS

10 x 8-inch rectangular baking sheet covered in plastic wrap

Sharp knife

1. In a small saucepan, bring the cream to a boil over a medium flame. Place the chocolate in a large bowl and pour the boiling cream over the chocolate to melt it. Add the Amaretto and whisk until smooth and uniform.

2. Divide the mixture evenly into two bowls. Add the muscadine to one bowl and mix well with a spatula. Pour the chocolate muscadine mixture onto the baking sheet and spread evenly with a rubber spatula. Freeze for 30 minutes.

3. Remove from the freezer and pour the rest of the chocolate mixture over the sheet. Spread the chocolate evenly with a rubber spatula. Freeze for 30 minutes.

4. Remove from the freezer and transfer to a work surface. Remove the plastic wrap from the chocolate to free the cold slab of chocolate. Cut the slab in half lengthwise with a sharp knife. Cut each section into 1/2-inch thick strips. Serve immediately or store in an airtight container in a cool dark place for up to 1 week.

See picture on opposite page.

BUTTER WHISKEY TRUFFLES

The best whiskey is aged in oak barrels for more than 20 years.

MAKES 30

3/4 cup heavy cream

10 ounces bittersweet chocolate

1/4 cup butter

1 tablespoon whiskey

1/4 cup premium cocoa

TOOLS

Pastry bag with 1/2-inch round tip

Disposable gloves

Baking paper

Baking sheet

1. In a small saucepan, bring the cream to a boil over a medium flame.

2. Place the chocolate in a large bowl and pour the boiling cream over the chocolate to melt it. Add the butter and whiskey and whisk until smooth and uniform.

3. Refrigerate for 30 minutes.

4. When the chocolate has cooled, transfer to the pastry bag. Pipe 1-inch rounds onto the baking paper 1/2-inch apart.

5. While wearing gloves, roll each round into a ball using the palms of your hands.

6. Roll each ball in the cocoa so that it is completely coated.

7. Place each ball on a baking sheet 1/2-inch apart. Let cool for 1 hour at room temperature until the chocolate hardens.

8. Serve immediately or store in an airtight container in a cool dark place for up to 2 weeks.

CHOCOLATE BALLS FOR KIDS

MAKES 30

7 ounces Petit Beurre cookies

2/3 cup sugar

1/2 cup cocoa

2/3 cup milk

1 teaspoon vanilla extract

1 cup butter, at room temperature

1/4 cup colored sprinkles (for decoration)

1/4 cup chocolate sprinkles (for decoration)

TOOLS

Large plastic zipper bag

Rolling pin

Small paper cupcake wrappers

Prepare this recipe for your child's birthday party and the partygoers will love the fun of making their own candy.

1. Place the cookies in a plastic zipper bag that is large enough to hold all the cookies without being totally filled. Close the bag.

2. Crush the cookies with a rolling pin to form crumbs the size of grains of rice.

3. Place the crumbs in a bowl, add the sugar and the cocoa and mix well.

4. Add the milk, vanilla, and butter and stir well.

5. Place the colored sprinkles in one shallow dish and the chocolate sprinkles in another dish.

6. Take heaping spoonfuls of the mixture and roll small balls using the palms of your hands.

7. Roll half the balls in colored sprinkles and half in chocolate sprinkles.

8. Place each ball in a cupcake wrapper and arrange on a tray to serve. The balls can be stored in an airtight container for up to 2 days.

You can use shaved coconut, powdered sugar, or any kind of decoration.

6

COLD AND HOT DRINKS

CHOCOLATE MILKSHAKE

SERVES 4

4 ounces quality bittersweet chocolate

1/4 cup heavy cream

1 cup chocolate ice cream

2/3 cup cold milk

A refreshing classic with a gourmet touch.

1. Melt the chocolate in a double boiler.

2. When the chocolate is completely melted, add the cream and whisk until well mixed.

3. While the chocolate is melting, blend the ice cream and milk in a blender at high speed until they form a smooth, uniform mixture.

4. Coat the sides of a tall glass with half the melted chocolate mixture. Pour the blended ice cream and milk into the glass and pour the remaining chocolate on top. Serve immediately.

MOCHA MILKSHAKE

SERVES 4

1 cup chocolate ice cream

1/4 cup cold milk

1/3 cup quality coffee

Delicious pick-me-up for a hot summer's day.

1. Blend the ice cream and the milk in a blender at high speed for 2 minutes.

2. Add the coffee and continue to blend until the mixture is smooth and uniform.

3. Pour the mixture into a tall glass and serve immediately.

See picture on opposite page.

BANANA CHOCOLATE MILKSHAKE

SERVES 4
1 cup chocolate ice cream
1/3 cup cold milk
1 peeled, ripe banana

The word "banana" has its root in the Arabic word "banan", which means "finger".

1. Blend all the ingredients in a blender at high speed until the mixture is smooth and consistent.

2. Pour into a tall glass and serve immediately.

COCONUT CHOCOLATE MILKSHAKE

SERVES 4
1 cup chocolate ice cream
2/3 cup coconut milk
2 tablespoons coconut liqueur

Replacing regular milk with coconut milk gives this milkshake a unique tropical flavor.

1. Blend all the ingredients in a blender at high speed until the mixture is smooth and uniform.

2. Pour into a tall glass and serve immediately.

FROZEN CHOCOLATE

SERVES 4
1 cup chocolate ice cream
1/4 cup cold milk
1/2 cup ice cubes

This frozen treat is another variation of the classic milkshake.

1. Blend all the ingredients in a blender at high speed until the mixture is smooth and consistent.

2. Pour into a tall glass and serve immediately.

See picture on opposite page.

CHOCOLATE MILK

SERVES 4

3 tablespoons premium cocoa

1/4 cup sugar

2 cups cold milk

This is a children's favorite all over the world. Prepare this with love and your kids will thank you.

1. In a small saucepan combine the sugar, cocoa, and half a cup of milk and whisk well. While stirring constantly, heat the mixture over a low flame until it comes to a boil.

2. Once the mixture has boiled, remove from the heat and add the remaining milk. Mix well and chill in the refrigerator for 1 hour.

3. After the chocolate milk has cooled, serve immediately or store in the refrigerator for up to 2 days. Mix well before serving.

See picture on opposite page.

CIOCCOLATA (ITALIAN HOT CHOCOLATE)

SERVES 4

2 tablespoons premium cocoa

1/4 cup sugar

1 cup cold milk

1 cup heavy cream

5 ounces bittersweet chocolate

Warm and comforting, this drink is perfect for enjoying with your favorite biscotti.

1. In a small saucepan, combine the cocoa, sugar, and half a cup of milk. Whisk well until all the cocoa is completely combined with the milk.

2. Add the remaining milk and the cream and bring to a boil over a low flame while stirring.

3. After the milk comes to a boil, add the chocolate and whisk well until the chocolate is completely melted and the mixture is uniform.

4. Serve hot in demitasse cups.

RICH HOT CHOCOLATE

SERVES 4

2 cups heavy cream

1/4 cup sugar

7 ounces bittersweet chocolate

This decadent hot chocolate drink will indulge your sweet tooth.

1. In a small saucepan, combine the cream and sugar. Bring to a boil over a low flame while stirring.

2. After the cream comes to a boil, add the chocolate and whisk until the chocolate is melted and the mixture is uniform.

3. Serve hot in demitasse cups.

HOT CHOCOLATE WITH WHIPPED CREAM

This luscious drink brings to mind cold winters in front of a cozy fireplace.

1. In a small saucepan, combine the cocoa, sugar, and half a cup of milk. Whisk well until all the cocoa is completely combined with the milk.

2. Add the remaining milk and the cream and bring to a boil over a low flame while stirring.

3. After the milk comes to a boil, add the chocolate and whisk well until the chocolate is completely melted and the mixture is uniform.

4. While the chocolate is melting, whip the whipping cream together with the two tablespoons of sugar until it forms stiff peaks. (You can use an electric mixer or whisk by hand to whip the cream.)

5. To serve, pour the hot chocolate into large mugs and top with a heaping spoonful of whipped cream.

CHOCOLAT CHAUD (FRENCH HOT CHOCOLATE)

Rich, hot, and creamy – on a lazy Sunday afternoon, sip this rich indulgence and imagine you are relaxing in Paris.

1. In a small saucepan, combine the cocoa, sugar, and half a cup of milk. Whisk well until all the cocoa is completely combined with the milk.

2. Add the remaining milk and the cream and bring to a boil over a low flame while stirring.

3. Serve hot in demitasse cups.

See picture on opposite page.

VIENNESE COFFEE

SERVES 4
4 ounces bittersweet chocolate
1 cup heavy cream
2 cups fresh hot strong coffee, preferably espresso
1/3 cup sugar
1 tablespoon fine cocoa
1/2 teaspoon cinnamon

A warm and enticing traditional coffee drink.

1. Melt the chocolate in the top of a double boiler.
2. After the chocolate has melted, add half the cream and whisk well while still in the double boiler.
3. Remove from the heat and pour the coffee into the chocolate.
4. Whip the remaining cream and the sugar with an electric mixer until it forms very soft peaks.
5. Fill mugs halfway with coffee and chocolate mixture.
6. Pour the cream on the coffee and, using a fine mesh, sprinkle a small amount of cocoa and cinnamon on top of each mug of coffee.
7. Serve immediately.

SPICED HOT CHOCOLATE

SERVES 4
2/3 cup heavy cream
1 cup cold milk
1/2 teaspoon ground cinnamon
1/2 teaspoon ground cloves
1/4 cup sugar
6 ounces bittersweet chocolate
1 tablespoon brandy

This is hot chocolate with a spicy kick.

1. In a small saucepan, combine the cream, milk, cinnamon, cloves, and sugar, and bring to a boil over a low flame while stirring.
2. After the milk comes to a boil, add the chocolate and brandy. Whisk well until the chocolate is completely melted and the mixture is uniform.
3. Serve hot in demitasse cups.

See picture on opposite page.